I0011162

Samsung Galaxy Note 3 User Manual

The Ultimate Guide for Mastering Your Galaxy Note 3

Just got your hands on the new Galaxy Note 3?

Learn what most owners of this NEW PHABLET don't… and transform this powerful device into your ultimate entertainment and productivity machine!

By
Daniel Forrester
Author & Tech Enthusiast

Table of Contents

Introduction

Whether you call your Galaxy Note 3 a phone, tablet, phablet, or something in between, this device is incredibly powerful when used properly and efficiently. It provides substantial improvements over the Galaxy Note 2, and outshines most other smartphones on the market today.

Samsung has combined a superior beautiful faux leather exterior, high quality screen, intuitive functionalities, and a wealth of applications to craft the ultimate all-inclusive device.

The Note 3 is competitively priced and available for a host of different data carriers. The Samsung Galaxy Note 3 is leaps and bounds above the competition in terms of quality, features, and innovation.

This guide was created to help the average consumer become an extraordinary and efficient Note 3 user.

Today's devices, especially the Note 3, demand a certain learning curve. Reading this guide will shorten such learning curve, and this guide itself will become a dependable reference for all future use of your device.

Chapter 1: What's in the Box?

The Samsung Galaxy Note 3 is the latest byproduct of Android's evolutionary smartphone venture.

The design is substantially different from the Note 2, the previous device in this line. The Note 3 is much more thin and lighter in weight, making it a more practical device for using and carrying around.

Inside the box for the Galaxy Note 3, you will find the following:

- Samsung Galaxy Note 3 Handset
- Battery
- Charger Plug Connector
- USB Cable
- Earphones
- Warranty Card
- Quick Start Guide

First, we will look at the impressive technical specs the phone offers and then we will quickly review the comparison between your Note 3 and the previous Note 2. Lastly, we will look at the layout of your new device.

Galaxy Note 3 Technical Specs

Feature	Specs
OS	Android
Physical Specification	151.2 x 79.2 x 8.3 mm Dimension 168 g Weight
Display	FHD AMOLED Technology 16 M Color Depth 5.7" Size

	1920 x 1080 Resolution S Pen
Memory	32GB Memory
Network	GSM | HSPA+ support GSM / GPRS / EDGE (850 / 900 / 1.800 / 1.900 MHz) support HSPA+ (850 / 900 / 1.900 / 2.100 MHz) support 802.11a/b/g/n/ac available Wi-Fi Direct available Bluetooth 4.0: PBAP, A2DP, AVRCP, HFP, HSP, OPP, SAP, HID, PAN, DI, MAP NFC available DLNA, MHL 2.0 support KIES, KIES Air support
Chipset	OCTA available Big Core 1,9 GHz Quad + Little core 1,3 GHz Quad GHz CPU Speed
Sensors	Accelerometer, Geomagnetic, Gyro, RGB light, Barometer, Proximity, Gesture, Temperature & Humidity, Hall available
Connectors	USB 2.0, USB 3.0 (MTP only) 3,5 mm Stereo Earjack MicroSD External Memory Slot (up to 64 GB) Micro SIM (3 FF) support Micro USB 3.0 (5,3 V, 2 A) Available MHL available
Services and Applications	Samsung Apps available Available in Samsung Hub (dependent on market) ChatON available

	ActiveSync available EAS / MDM / ODE / VPN
Battery	3.200 mAh Standard Battery Up to 11 H Internet Usage Time (3G) Up to 13 H Internet Usage Time (Wi-Fi) Up to 12 H Video Playback Time Up to 68 H Audio Playback Time 3.200 mAh battery Capacity USB Chargeable Up to 20 H Talk Time (W-CDMA) Up to 490 H Standby Time (W-CDMA)
Audio and Video	Video Format: MP4, M4V, 3GP, WMV, ASF, AVI, FLV, MKV, WEBMVideo Codec: MPEG4, H.263, H.264, VC-1, VP8, MP43, WMV7 / 8, Sorenson Spark, HEVC Full HD (1080p) Video Playback available Recording up to 60 fps Format: MP3, AAC, OGA, WAV, WMA, AMR, AWB, FLAC, XMF, MXMF, IMY, RTTTL, RTX, OTACodec : MP3, AAC, AAC+, eAAC+, AMR-WB, AMR-NB, FLAC, WMA, WAV
Camera	CMOS, 2 MP Megapixels Camera Resolution(Front) CMOS, 13 MP Megapixels Camera Resolution (Rear) Power HCRI LED (1 EA) Flash

7

	Auto Focus available
Color	Jet Black, Classic White, Blush Pink
Location	Assisted GPS, GLONASS

Galaxy Note 2 vs. Galaxy Note 3

While the technical specs are certainly impressive, the best way to get a real appreciation for the device is with a comparison to the Galaxy Note 2.

The Design

One of the biggest differences, and one that is immediately noticeable, is the design and appearance of the phone.

Instead of the traditionally smooth and shiny plastic casing, the new phone utilizes a plastic casing that has the look and the feel of faux leather. This provides the phone with a drastically different look from the Galaxy Note 2. The phone has a durable appearance and the faux leather helps to provide you with a better grip, as well as helping to prevent smudges and fingerprints.

The Galaxy Note 3 weighs in at only 168 grams, which is 15 grams lighter than it's predecessor. It is also 1mm thinner than the Note 2.

The Display

The Galaxy Note 3 boasts a beautiful 5.7" Full HD Super AMOLED display. It is capable of producing a resolution of 1920 x 1080 at 386ppi. The colors are vibrant and the phone's screen provides excellent viewing angles.

The Galaxy Note 2 has a 5.5" Super AMOLED screen with a resolution of just 720 x 1280 at 267ppi.

The higher pixel count on the Note 3 allows the graphics and text displayed on the phone to have a sharper appearance. The Galaxy Note 2 is unable to provide the same amount of graphical detail and clarity.

Camera

The Galaxy Note 3 features a 13-megapixel rear camera that takes great shots, and can shoot fairly well in low light (something most smartphone cameras and even regular cameras have difficulties with). The Galaxy Note 2 features only an 8-megapixel camera.

The camera offers a number of built-in filters and effects, and allows for photos as well as 1080p videos shot at 60 frames per second. It can capture 4K video at 30 frames per second. The camera also offers 120 frames per second for slow motion, although it loses some of the sharpness at this setting.

Battery

The Note 3 features a 3200 mAh Li-ion battery that is just a bit larger than the Li-ion 3100 in the Note 2. The Note 3's battery can last approximately the same amount of time as the Note 2's battery. Third party testing shows that the phone's battery offers an estimated six hours and eight minutes of power in typical real life situations.

Software

The Note 3 offers much more in terms of the software than the Note 2 does. It has all of the same software features found in the recently released Samsung Galaxy S4, as well as some new and powerful additions to the software that includes Pen Window and Air Command.

Layout – The Note 3 Exterior

The front facing button layout matches that of the Galaxy Note 2 and should be familiar to those who have used other phones in this line.

The Galaxy Note 3 features a home button located directly below the screen, as well as capacitive touch 'back' and 'menu' buttons. It is possible to operate the capacitive touch buttons with a fingertip or with the S Pen. The power button is on the right side of the phone and the volume button is on the left side, which is the same as with the Note 2.

The back of the Note 3 is removable. Beneath the cover are the slots for the SIM card, microSD cards, as well as the battery.

Turning On Your Note 3

The power button is located on the right side of the phone. Press and hold the button to turn the device on. To turn it off, press and hold the button again and then tap "Power Off". If the Note 3 ever freezes, stops, or has fatal errors, press and hold the power button for at least seven seconds in order to reset the device.

You can also press the power button to lock or unlock the device. The device will go into "lock mode" once the touch screen turns off.

Powering On/Off & Sleep Mode

A single press of the power button can wake the Note 3 or put the phone back to sleep. The phone is always technically "on" so it can receive incoming phone calls *unless* you deliberately hold the power button for several seconds to turn it off.

A long press of the power button will bring up a screen that gives you the option to turn the power off entirely, restart the phone, or put it into Airplane mode. Other options appear on the screen as well:

Mute – Stops the device from making any noises and stops vibrating.

Vibrate – Allows the phone to vibrate, but the phone will not make any sounds through the speaker.

Sound – This setting allows the phone to vibrate as well as play sounds.
In addition to these sound settings, it is important to note that the Note 3 also has four different types of settings for volume:

Ringtone – This controls the volume of the sound that plays whenever you have an incoming call.

Media – Controls the audio volume of the sound that plays while using video apps, music apps, and playing games.

Notifications – This controls volume of the alerts played whenever you have an incoming text, email, or other alert.

System – This controls the audio for a variety of phone features, including the touch sounds, the sound of the keypad, and more.

The volume control buttons on the left side of the phone control both the Media and Ringtone volumes; the function of these buttons depend on what you happen to be doing with the phone at the time.

Registering Your Device

Register your device through the Samsung website: http://www.samsung.com/us/support/register/product.

Samsung usually offers discounts and coupons for those who register their Samsung devices.

Deregister

Deregistering, or unregistering a device is again made possible via Samsung.

Whenever selling or getting rid of a phone of any type, you should reset the device and remove all files and information from the phone. Additionally, you also may want to remove the SIM card if being extra cautious.

Navigating Your Note 3

Every Note 3 owner should take his or her time in simply getting use to this new device before trying any advanced maneuvers.

Learning the basic layout and the functions of the various buttons helps to reduce the learning curve and eliminates the experimenting phase most users endure.

Basic Buttons (Home, Menu, Back Buttons)

Home Button

The home button is located on the front of the phone just below the screen. It can serve different functions based on how you tap it.

- When on any screen other than the home page, a single tap of the home button will return you to the home screen.

- Tapping the button once when you are already on the home screen will open My Magazine.

- A double-tap of the home button will open S Voice.

Holding the home button, regardless of the screen you are on at the time, will bring up the task switcher so you can switch between different tasks.

Menu and Back Buttons

The phone's menu and back buttons are not physical buttons. They are capacitive touch buttons, meaning you can tap them with a finger or by using your S Pen. The menu button is left of the home button, and the back button is to the right. They are only visible when the screen is backlit.

The menu button will bring up a menu for whichever app happens to be open at the time, as long as that particular app has a menu.

The back button will take you to the previous screen in most cases. However, it will sometimes have other functions. For example, if the onscreen keyboard is open, pressing the back button will hide it.

Your Home Screen

Your home screen is the basic "starting area" for your Android phone. The home screen serves a similar function to that of computer's desktop. The icons that you see on the home screen are shortcuts to various apps. Opening these apps gives you access to the content of the app (media, utility, documents, files, etc.).

Navigating Your Home Screen

The phone also has more than just one home screen. By swiping to the left or right, it is possible for you to navigate to other, secondary home screens that have other apps and widgets on them. The purpose of multiple home screens is to just give you more space to add shortcuts for apps/utilities to save you time, and also to provide more space for the organizational purposes.

Landscape Mode

Landscape mode will work with most apps, including the home screen, App Drawer, and notification panel, as well as most downloaded apps. To put the phone into landscape mode, you simply have to turn it sideways. The phone will then automatically convert what is on the screen to the wider landscape appearance.

Entering Text

One of the most basic functions of using the Galaxy Note 3 is entering text. You have three different ways you can input the text.

- Keyboard

- S Pen

- Voice

Keyboard

The keyboard is the default method used for entering text into the Note 3. The phone includes a standard touch keyboard, although it is possible to download alternatives for advanced users who may want to have different features included in their keyboard.

The included keyboard is easily accessible and fast. The Note 3 is also compatible with external keyboards if desired.

By tapping the shift key on the keyboard, you enable/disable caps lock for creating uppercase/lowercase letters and different symbols. Tapping and holding a character key will open the secondary characters that are featured on each of the keys. Some keys have several secondary characters you can access in this way. The "sym" key will switch between the standard keys and the symbols.

As you type, the Note 3 predicts the words being typed in the black bar just above the keyboard. Tapping the word will choose it, which can help save a lot of typing.

Voice

To activate voice input, tap the microphone key located to the right of the "sym" key on the keyboard. This will bring up an input screen, and you can then begin speaking and dictating. You can tap the red microphone icon to pause the dictation, or you can tap the dropdown menu located just above the icon to change languages. Tapping the microphone once more will resume the dictation.

Tapping the keyboard silhouette will return the phone to the keyboard setting.

S Pen

The third way to input text into the Note 3 is with the S Pen. Pressing and holding the
microphone button on the keyboard brings up a small screen with several options:

- Activate voice input
- Activate handwriting recognition mode
- Show recent clipboard items
- Keyboard settings
- Emoticons
- Keyboard type

When using the S Pen, input the text by tapping on the keyboard with the pen, as you might with your fingers, or activate the handwriting recognition mode, which will allow you to use the pen as a normal pen, "writing" on the screen. The Note 3 then translates that writing into text.

Home Screen Customization

By default, Samsung places several shortcuts on the initial homepage. These include Email, Calendar, Camera, and S Note.

Below that, you will see a house, which represents the home screen, with dashes to either side. When the house is white, it indicates that you are on the main home screen. Those dashes represent the secondary and adjacent home screens. You can switch to the other home screens by swiping left or right.

Below the indicator for the home screen is the App Tray. The tray is where you can put the apps you use the most or that are most important to you. The apps in the App Tray will be visible on all of the home screens. The default settings for the App Tray from Samsung are Phone, Contacts, Messages, Internet, and Apps. However, you can customize the home screens to your liking.

Customization of the home screen from the factory settings is relatively easy for you to do. One of the simplest methods of customization is to tap and hold the shortcut you want to rearrange and then drag it to a new location.

In addition to rearranging apps and widgets, you can also remove them. Again, tap and hold, and then drag the app or widget to the "remove" bar that appears. Once you drag it into place, simply release it. This is helpful for those who need to free up more room on the screen.

For the apps located in the App Tray, it is possible to move and remove them in the same manner as all of the other apps and widgets on the Note 3, by tapping, holding, and dragging.

The menu button on the home screen also provides options if you are customizing your screen. Tapping the menu will bring up six different options.

Add apps and widgets – Tapping this will bring you to the App Drawer.

17

Create folder – Tapping the "create folder" option allows you to create and name a folder on the home screen. You can then place other app shortcuts into the folder.

Set wallpaper – This option allows you to customize and set your own background images for the home screens. To change the wallpaper, go to the home screen, and tap and hold on an empty space. This brings up a set of options, including the option to set wallpaper. Choose from an image in your Gallery, or download from the web and save it to your Gallery. You can choose to apply the wallpaper to your home screen, lock screen, or both.

Edit page – The "edit page" option allows you to rearrange home screens by tapping and dragging.

Settings – Tapping this option opens up the screen for all of the Note 3 settings.
Help – The "help" option opens up a tutorial to teach you about the Note 3.

Status Bar

At the top of the screen is a horizontal black area that serves as the status bar. The status bar indicates a variety of things including:

- Current time
- Battery/charging indicator
- Cell signal strength
- Wi-Fi signal strength
- Smart Stay indicator

Directly beneath the status bar is a widget that shows the local weather, the date, and the time. Below that is generally a Google search bar to make searching the web fast and easy.

Notification Panel

Access the notification panel by placing your finger on the status bar and then swiping down. The Note 3 places important information and notifications in this panel, and will allow you fast access to a number of settings.

At the top of the panel are the time and the date, as well as two symbols – a gear and several squares. Tapping the gear will open up the device settings, which is the same screen you will find if you activate settings from the home screen menu. The squares will open up the settings for the toggle buttons, which are the set of buttons just below.

These buttons include Wi-Fi, Sound, Bluetooth, GPS, and more. They are called toggle buttons because they have an on or off setting that you can toggle based on your need.

You can also drag the notification panel down with two fingers to reveal the various toggle buttons available, or swipe to the left to access the second row of toggle buttons.

Note that by swiping left, you can only access the second row, not any of the subsequent rows of toggle buttons.

Below the toggle buttons on the notification screen is a brightness selector for the screen, which you can adjust manually. You could also check the "auto" box, and this automatically changes the level of brightness for the screen based on your surroundings.

The main function of the notification screen is to notify you of text messages, missed phone calls, notices from apps, and other notifications. Tapping on the notifications will trigger an action. If you have a text message in the notifications screen and tap on it, the

Note 3 will open the Messages app, so you can then respond.

Hitting the "clear" button will clear all of the notifications without needing to tap them. It is also possible to clear just a single notification without tapping on it simply by swiping it to the left or the right.

It is important to note that deleting a notification does nothing to the actual action you are being notified about. For example, clearing a notification about a new message won't delete that message. You will still find that new message in your messages inbox; the notification will be the only thing removed.

The App Drawer

The App Drawer contains all of the apps installed on the Note 3. To open the App Drawer, click on the "apps" shortcut located in the App Tray. This opens up a screen that has a button for apps on one side and widgets on the other side. This provides access to all of the apps and widgets, while the most important ones are the ones you place on the home screens and secondary screens.

The Apps Tab

The Apps tab in the App Drawer stores the apps on the device. This is where you can find your apps and create shortcuts for them on your home screen. By tapping and holding an app in the drawer, it shows a silhouetted image of the home screen and lets you copy the shortcut to your screen as long as there is room. It is also possible to add a new shortcut to the App Drawer in this manner.

By tapping the menu key while in the apps tab, it reveals a number of options.

Edit – You can customize the App Drawer. You can rearrange the order of the apps, drag an app to the menu to create folders, page, or app, and drag the app to the info option to learn more about the app. You can also drop the app into a previously created folder. After making changes, tap "save" to make sure the changes save to the Note 3.

Create Folder – Tapping this option allows you to create a folder, just like you can do for the home screen.

View Type – This option allows you to change the way the device sorts the apps in the drawer, making them easier to find.

Uninstall/Disable – This option brings up a screen that allows you to tap the apps to remove them from the device, or to disable the apps.

Show Disabled Apps – This option lets you see any disabled apps on the Note 3.

The Lock Screen

You want to keep data and information protected from theft and from prying eyes. The lock screen can help with that, and it is one of the best and simplest ways to keep information safe.

The lock screen generally activates whenever the Note 3 goes to sleep. The lock screen stops people from accessing the Note 3 until they input the correct user authentication, which is generally in the form of a PIN. However, some may want to use pattern recognition or signature recognition with the S Pen.

To set up a lock screen, go to Device Settings, then Device, and then Lock Screen and choose from one of the settings. Choose from the following.

Swipe – This setting does not offer any real security, as it only stops the screen from activating until someone swipes it.

Signature – The signature setting will require you to unlock the Note 3 by signing your name on the lock screen with the S Pen. You will have a PIN backup if you do not have the S Pen.

Pattern – The pattern option lets you create a special pattern on a 3x3 grid, which you have to input to bypass the lock screen. This also has PIN as a backup.
PIN – The PIN method requires a PIN to unlock the phone. The PIN has a 4-digit minimum, but no maximum.

Password – The password option works similarly to the PIN, but it makes use of letters, numbers, and special characters rather than just numbers.
None – Some choose this option to do away with a lock screen entirely. This is the least safe method.

Motions & Gestures

The Note 3 also offers motion and gesture controls. Enabling motions requires going into the device settings, then controls, and then motions. If the slider is off, tap it to turn on motions. You will see five different motion options that you can then turn on or off with sliders.

Here are the motion controls:

Direct Call – When you are looking at a contact's details, details from a message, or call details from the call log, placing the Note 3 to the ear will initiate a phone call.
Smart Alert – When picking up the Note 3, it will automatically tell you if there are any messages or missed calls.

Zoom – Turning on the zoom motion control lets you touch and hold two spots on the screen when viewing a website or picture. You can then tilt the device back and forth in order to zoom in and out.

Browse Image – When viewing a zoomed in picture, it is possible to touch a point on the screen and then move the device left, right, up, or down to pan the image.

Mute/Pause – With this motion control active, you can turn over the Note 3 as a method of muting incoming calls and pausing media.

Smart Screen Features

The Note 3 has features that make use of the front camera to observe your face and then perform certain actions. To enable these features go to device settings, then controls, and then to smart screen, and turn them on by tapping.

Smart Stay – This keeps the screen on as long as you look at it, even if there is a timeout setting on the device.

Smart Rotation – This will rotate the screen according to the orientation of your face rather than using the gravity sensor.

Smart Pause – When you look away from a video, the device will pause. This works in
YouTube apps and Video apps.

Smart Scroll – The camera will detect your head movement as a means to scroll webpages and lists. This will only work with email apps and the Internet.

Widgets

Widgets are different from apps, and are only used on the home screen. A widget can be any size and could contain many different types of content. Removing a widget from a home screen is the same as removing an app. Tap and hold the widget, and then drag it to the "remove" area.

In the App Drawer, there is a tab for widgets just as there is for apps. This shows all of the widgets on the device. The Note 3 has a number of widgets already installed, including clocks, weather widgets, finance widgets, a YouTube widget and more. You can add them to your home screen by tapping and holding, just as you would add an app.

While in the widgets tab, the menu key will display two options.

Search – This option allows people to filter the widgets on display by name and works like a traditional search feature.

Uninstall – The uninstall feature lets you remove third-party widgets from the Note 3.

The widgets you can remove will have a red minus symbol next to your name; some widgets that come with the phone will not be able to be removed.

S Pen

The S Pen, located at the bottom right side of the Galaxy Note 3, is a tool that provides users of the Note 3 even more functionality. It is useful for handwriting messages and texts, and much more. The redesign from the Note 2's pen is readily noticeable, and the new pen works well with the upgraded, higher quality screen of the Note 3.

Air Command, which you can activate when removing the S Pen, acts as a route to reach all of the various functions of the pen. It allows you to go into Action Memo,

Scrapbooker, Screen Write, S Finder, and Pen Window quickly and easily. You can also access this menu by hovering over the screen and clicking the button on the side of the pen.

Scrapbooker – You can use the stylus to draw around part of the screen to take a screenshot. You can add text, notes, and categories to organize the images, which go to the Scrapbook app on the Note 3.

Screen Write – This allows you to take a screenshot of your current page and then write notes on the image. It is possible to change the pen size and ink color by tapping the pen icon in the upper left portion of the screen. On the right is an eraser, undo and redo tools, crop options, as well as share, cancel, and save.

S Finder – This option allows you to search for anything on your devices, such as apps or contacts.

Pen Window – This option lets you draw a box on your screen and then launch one of the following apps inside of the box: Browser, Calculator, ChatOn, Clock, Contacts, Hangouts, Phone, YouTube.

Multi Window

Multi Window works very similarly to Pen Window, but it will split the screen into two sections that sit next to one another. This feature lets you open two apps at the same time, and you can do this in both portrait and landscape mode.

Pull down the notifications panel and make sure the toggle button for Multi Window shows that the option is on and then back out of the panel. A long press of the back button will launch the Multi Window mode. At the left side of the screen, you will see a tab you can hold and drag open. This shows the apps that Multi Window will work with and allows you to tap on the app to open it and split the screen.

Make a Call

To make a call of then Note 3, you will use the phone app located in the App Tray. Tap the shortcut, which opens up a number of options for making phone calls.

Keypad

You can tap the keypad and dial the outgoing number just as you would with a traditional phone. After entering the number, go to the green button under the zero key and tap it to dial.

Logs

The log button lets you look at the recent incoming and outgoing calls. You can make a call by tapping the number of the contact and then the green button to dial.

Favorites

The favorites tab shows the numbers you contacts most frequently. Tap the contact or number and then the green button to dial.

Contacts

The contacts tab allows you to view all of the contacts in the phone book. Again, you will tap the contact name and then the green button to make the call.

Answer a Call

To answer a call, tap and hold the green phone icon that is on the screen and then drag it to the right.

Reject a Call

If you want to reject a call for whatever reason, you can tap and hold the red phone icon on the screen and drag it to the left. Another method of rejecting the call is to swipe the tab at the bottom of the phone that says, "reject call with message".

Swiping upward will reject the call and send a text message to the caller!

You can create a custom message by tapping the button for create new message.

Alternatively, you can go to settings, and then device, then call, then set up call rejection messages. This message will be your default rejection message. Use this option if you wish to save time and avoid writing a custom message for every response.

Overseas Calling

When dialing overseas, the U.S. dialing needs to be disabled in order to access the international dialing code. Press the home button and then the menu button. Go into the settings and then device.

Tap call and then tap the check box next to U.S. dialing, and this will disable the setting. Then tap international dialing and use the keypad to enter the international dialing code. Finally, tap OK, and this will save the code.

Speed Dialing

To create a speed dialing contact, go to the phone app and tap on the keypad tab. Then tap on the menu button and finally tap on the tab for speed dial setting. From there, tap on the number you want to assign to the contact and then select the contact.

When speed dialing, simply go to the keypad and tap the assigned number of the person you want to call. If you assign a friend to speed dial "2", simply hold "2" and the phone will dial. If someone is assigned "15", tap the one and then hold the "5" to make the call.

To remove or reassign a setting, go to the speed dial setting, and tap on the contact you want removed and then select whether to remove or reassign.

In-Call Options

During a phone call, you have a number of different options that appear on screen.

Add call/Merge – Tapping add call will dial a new number and set up a multiparty call for up to three people. After establishing the other call, tap on merge to form the multiparty call.

Keypad/Hide – Displays or hides the keypad.
End Call – Tapping the button will end the current call.

Speaker – This will switch the audio between the speaker on the phone and the earpiece. You can adjust the volume of the call with the volume button.

Mute/Un-mute – Tapping this will turn the microphone on or off, which can stop parties on the other end of the call from hearing you or any background noses.

Headset – By tapping headset, you can switch the audio from the speaker or earpiece to a Bluetooth headset paired with the device.

You can also tap the menu for more options:

Contacts – Tapping this will add the number to your contacts.

Action Memo – Tapping the button lets you create a note with Action Memo.

Message – Opens up the message app to send a message.

One-handed Operation On/Off – This allows you to turn on or off the one-handed operation mode.

Checking Voicemail

To check voicemail, go to the phone app and tap the keypad tab. Then, tap the icon beneath the * key that looks like a cassette tape and follow the onscreen prompts to listen to the message.

When first calling voicemail, you may need to set your PIN and greeting. This can differ based on the carrier.

Visual Voicemail

Some carriers offer a visual voicemail app in the App Drawer. This shows the voicemails in a list on the screen so you do not have to use number commands to handle your voicemail messages.

Sending a Text Message

Text messages go through the messages app on the Note 3, which is in the App Tray and the App Drawer. After opening the app, tap on the pen and paper icon in the top right part of the screen. This lets you compose a new message.

Choose the message recipient by typing a name or phone number into the field at the top of the screen that reads, "Enter recipient". Another option is to tap on the button to the right of this field and select a contact from your phone book. It is possible to enter multiple recipients.

Then, enter your message in the message field. Once the message is complete, and you've added any additional media, click the envelope icon to send it.

Messages with Pictures, Video, and More

Enter your message in the message field and tap the paperclip icon to choose the additional media to send. It is possible to attach other media files, such as images, videos, and even voice recordings.

Once the message is complete, and you've added any additional media, click the envelope button to send the file.

Responses to text messages will show up in the notification panel, as well as in the messages app. You can tap the entry in the messages app, or the notification panel, which will then open up the thread.

Managing Your Contacts

The contacts app is essentially the Note 3's phonebook. It contains the names, numbers, email addresses, and other pertinent information about family, friends, and business associates.

Accessing Your Contacts

You can access the contacts app via several ways. It is in the App Tray by default, but you can access it by opening the phone app and tapping on the contacts tab. This tab is in the upper right corner of the screen after opening the phone app.

Search for a Contact

To search for a contact, you can tap a letter along the right edge of the screen to skip to the contacts that fall under that letter. You can also swipe up and down to scroll through the contacts, or type a name into the search bar. Tap on the contact to bring up the details.

Contact Options

Adding a Contact

To add a contact, tap the + icon located next to the search box and select the account in which you want to store the contact. Keeping them all connected to the Google account helps to ensure they are all in the same place, making it easy to restore all of them if necessary.

Enter the contact's information and then tap the green + sign if you need to add more fields for more information. Tap the face icon to assign a photo or image to the contact from the Gallery.

Editing Contacts

Tap the contact to open the details. Then tap on the pencil icon located in the upper right portion of the screen. This allows you to edit the contact's information.

Deleting Contacts

To delete a contact, tap and hold the contact in the main list view. This brings up the option to delete the contact.

Sharing Contacts

To share a contact with someone else, tap and hold a contact in the main list view and then choose the option for share via, and choose with whom you want to share the contact as well as how you want to share.

Favorites

The favorites tab shows the contacts that you call most often. Tapping on the tab is a fast way of getting to the contacts you want to call.

Linking and Synchronizing Contacts

Merging duplicate contacts in the contact database is possible by opening your Gmail account on the PC. Open the contacts, and use the Find & Merge Duplicates feature.

This helps to link the duplicate contacts you have on the Google servers.

However, this will not help when duplicate entries are created through other apps. To link *those*, you can use the link contact feature on the Note 3.

To use the feature, tap and hold the contact in your contact list and then select the option for link contact.

Chapter 5: Basic Features

This chapter covers the basic features of the Note 3 and how to operate them.

Swiping to Type

Another way to enter text into the Note 3 is through swiping, which can be much faster than traditional typing, although it does have a learning curve to it. You can swipe and type by placing a finger on the first letter of the word you want to spell and then move from letter to letter without lifting your finger.

On the Note 3, you will see the path your finger is taking as a blue line. It is possible to swipe with a finger as well as with an S Pen. On the Note 3, it is actually possible to swipe multiple words without lifting the finger.

While it takes time to get used to swiping, it can greatly speed up the process of typing.

Using Voice Recognition

Dictation into the Note 3 is possible through voice recognition. To activate the voice input, bring up the keyboard and tap the microphone key once. Then, start speaking to dictate. Voice recognition does more than just dictation though. It is also possible to dial contacts with your voice by saying their name.

How to Copy & Paste

Copying and pasting with the Note 3 is easy. Tap and hold the text or image you want to copy. Make sure the blue tabs surround the area that you want to copy and then tap copy. You can also swipe left and right in the toolbar for more options.

After copying the text, tap and hold on the area where you want to paste the text and then tap paste.

To access data previously copied, you can tap on the clipboard and then choose the data you want to place.

Connecting to Wi-Fi

Many times, you will want to connect to a wireless network. Whether you are at home, the office, or a friend's house, using wireless Internet is a good way to reduce the amount of data the phone has to stream. This will reduce the chance of going over your allotted data amount for the month and save you money.

Head to the notification panel to make sure the Wi-Fi is enabled. Then go to device settings, connections, and Wi-Fi. This will bring up a list of networks. Choose the network to which you want to connect and then follow the on-screen prompts to connect to the network.

Using Your Browser

The Note 3 comes with two different browsers to access the web. The first browser is simply called Internet, and the second is the mobile option for Google Chrome. Tapping on either of these will open up the browser.

Google Chrome is the more robust of the two options, and it is very simple to use. When you open Chrome for the first time, you will have to read and accept their Terms of Service, and you can then sign into your Google account. Using Chrome will make it easier to sync data such as your contacts from your Google accounts to your Note 3.

Web Search

To search the web, you can enter the URL for the site you want to visit, or you can enter search terms into the same search box to come up with a list of results. Choose from the results of the search by tapping on the one you want to visit.

Opening a Tab

You can have more than one tab open at the same time, which is similar to a desktop browser. This lets you go between webpages quickly and easily. To see the different open tabs, or to open a new tab, tap the number in the upper right portion of the screen. Tap on new tab to open a tab, or tap on one of the tabs you already have open, if there are any.

Incognito Browsing

Sometimes, you may want to browse the web without leaving a trace of where you've been in your browsing history. This is possible with the Note 3 thanks to the incognito tab.

To browse privately, tap the menu and select new incognito tab. This tab will have a blue background and that lets you know that you can browse without worrying about your data being stored in the form of "cookies".

Viewing Tabs on Your PC

Having a desktop version of Google Chrome that is set to sync open tabs, which is available through the search engine's "Advanced Sync Settings". This allows the Note 3 and the PC to view the same tabs; again, this a great feature and benefit to using Chrome for your browser.

Gmail

The Note 3 has two apps from which you can send and receive emails. The first of these is the Gmail app, which is a good solution for anyone already using Gmail, as well as those who want to switch to it. This is the simplest option for email on the Note 3, but the second option is discussed later in the chapter.

Setting up Gmail

Before using the Gmail app for the first time, you need to set up a Google account on the Note 3 if you have not already done so. When launching the Gmail app for the first time, it will prompt you to set up an account at that time.

After configuring Gmail with the phone, you can access all of the normal features of your Gmail account.

Inbox and Browsing Email

When in the Gmail inbox, tapping on an email will open it and allow you to view and then reply to it. By swiping the email to the left or right, you can archive it.

You can tap and hold an email to enter the selection mode. You can then tap and hold other emails in order to select them too. After selecting the emails you want, you can use the icons at the top of the screen. The folder icon will archive the email, the trashcan deletes the email, the gray envelope will mark the mail as unread, and the red envelope returns to the inbox.

Tap the red envelope in the upper left part of the screen or swipe from left to right in order to open up the mail toolbar. You can scroll up and down on the toolbar to see the various accounts and folders from which you can choose.

Composing an Email

To compose a new email in Gmail, tap on the gray envelope icon in the upper right portion of the screen. If you are already viewing a message, there will be a reply button instead and you can tap the reply button to change the mode to reply, reply-all, and forward.

Composing the message as you would normally compose a text as mentioned before. Choose the recipient or recipients, and then add attachments if needed, and finally send the email.

Adding Attachments

Through the Gmail app, you can attach videos and pictures. With the mail composition open, tap on the menu button and then select the option you want, and then choose the file you want to add.

Offline Storage

The Note 3 stores messages from the last thirty days to the internal memory. To access older messages, it contacts the Google servers and brings up the messages from offline storage.

It is possible to increase the number of days of mail stored on the phone for those who may not always have a viable connection. Go to the Gmail settings, then into your account and then tap the section for days of mail to sync. You can change the number of days there.

Gmail Options

Gmail offers a variety of different options that you may wish to consider using.

Email Notifications – When receiving several emails in a short period, the notification alert will only sound one time. Some may want to have alerts for all of your emails. To do this, go into the Gmail settings, then your account, inbox sound & vibrate, and check "notify for every message".

Disable Swipe to Archive – to disable the swipe to archive, go to Gmail settings, general settings, and then disable the "swipe to archive" setting.

Auto Fit Messages – Go to Gmail Settings, general settings and enable the feature to ensure the messages always fit properly on the Note 3's screen.

Add a Signature – To create a signature for all of the emails sent from your device, go to Gmail settings, your account, and then signature.

Confirm – This makes you confirm that you are sending a message to people before you actually send it, which can prevent messages from going to the wrong people. Go to Gmail settings, general settings, and enable "confirm before sending".

Using the Email App (Non Gmail)

The other email option on the Note 3 is for those who use non-Gmail accounts. The email features support for POP3 and IMAP mailboxes.

The app will work with a variety of email providers. When you click on the app and set it up, you will be able to enter your email address and password to the email. Click next and the app will attempt and most likely connect to the email.

You can then choose the settings for the email. Choose how often you want it to sync your email and whether you want notifications when emails are received. Finally, you can

39

choose an account name to use, as well as a name for the outgoing emails. Click on done and it will bring up the inbox.

From there, it is easy to access the account through the email app.

Using the Calendar

The calendar app that comes with the Note 3 is user friendly and provides you with a variety of different options. The calendar app is located in the App Drawer by default.

Calendar Navigation

When you tap on the calendar app and open it, you will see five different tabs located along the right side of the phone: Year, Month, Week, Day, List, Task.

Clicking on these different tabs will do different things. The tabs for year, month, week, and day will display exactly what they say – the year, month, etc. You can go into the year tab and then tap on any month in order to go directly to that month if you choose.

The year tab does not show events, but is helpful for navigating from one month to another quickly.

The list tab will show all of the upcoming events. The task tab is only tangentially related to the calendar, and we will discuss it in detail later in the chapter.

New Event

To create a new event, tap on the plus sign located in the upper right portion of the screen. That will take you to a new screen that will let you set up a new event. It has a number of options.

Title – Give the event a name and color code so it is easily recognizable in the calendar view.

All Day – Checking the button does not give the event any specific timeframe, and instead it shows up as all day, which lets other events in the day overlap with it if necessary.

From/To – You can set the start and end times and dates for the event.

Calendar – This lets you determine which calendar to save the event to. Selecting "My Calendar" saves the event to the Note 3, but will not sync it with Google. It may be better to select the calendar with the Google email address to ensure everything synchronizes.

Sticker – You can add a sticker to the event for easier identification when looking through your calendar.

Repeat – You can make the event recurring and determine the schedule.
Reminder – This setting will create an alarm for the event. You can choose a notification alarm that will sound on the Note 3 and will create a popup screen. The email type alarm will sent an email to your Google account.

Location – Enter a location name, or select a location using the maps app.

Description – Write a note about the event.

Participants – Add contacts from your contact list to the event if they are attending.

Show Me As – This is only important for you if you share your Google calendar with others. Changes to this setting will determine how the event displays for them.

Privacy – You can choose whether the event will be displayed on all shared calendars. Again, this is only important for those who are sharing your Google calendar.

New Task

Instead of adding a new event, you may want to add a new task. Tap the add task tap to the right of the add event tab at the top of the screen.

This opens up a screen that presents you with a variety of options and fields to fill out, some of which are similar to those for the new event.

Title – Create the name for the task, which is how it will appear in the task list.

Due Date – Set the deadline for the task. If there is no deadline, check the box for no due date.

Task – Choose the task list under which you will save the new task.

Reminder – Use this to set an alarm for the task. The same alarm settings (notification type and email type) are available for the reminder as they were for the new event.

Priority – Determine how urgent and important the task is.

Description – You can add a note about the task.

Managing Events/Tasks

When managing events and tasks, you will tap them once from the day or week mode of the calendar. Those who are in the month mode of the calendar will first have to tap the day and then tap the event.

Tapping will bring up the detailed view of the task or event.

Tap on the pencil icon in the upper right portion of the screen. This lets you edit the event or task, just as you did when creating it.

It is possible to share the task and event from the detail screen as well. Tap on the icon to the left of the pencil, or tap on the tab on the bottom of the screen that says forward.

From the detail view, it is possible to copy or delete events and tasks as well. Open up the menu button while in the detail view screen. This brings up the option to copy or delete.

Chapter 6: Using the Camera

The Note 3 features a 13-megapixel rear camera with an f/2.2 lens and a 1/3.06 sensor. It also features a 2-megapixel front camera. When using the camera app, it opens into the photo mode by default rather than the video mode.

Taking a Photo

When launching the camera app, you will see a number of buttons on the screen, each of which has a special function and which you need to understand in order to take good photos with your Note 3.

- At the bottom center of the screen is a camera icon, which is the shutter button. Press this when you want the camera to autofocus and take a photo.

- To the left of the shutter button is the mode button, which lets you sort through a number of different mode options, such as HDR, which we will discuss later.

- To the right of the shutter button is the video button. Again, that comes later in the chapter.

- Midway up on the left side of the screen is the white carat tab that, when opened, brings up a number of different effects, such as black and white.

- The camera and arrow icon in the upper right part of the screen lets you switch between the front and rear-facing cameras.

- The second icon from the top on the right side of the camera allows you to use both of the cameras at the same time in dual camera mode.

- The gear icon below the dual camera option brings up all of the settings for the camera.

- You can tap anywhere on the screen to change the point for autofocus.

Browsing Photos You've Taken

In the upper left part of the screen, you will see a thumbnail. Tapping on this thumbnail will let you look at the photos you've recently taken by bringing them to the Gallery app.

Shooting Video

To the right of the camera shutter button on the screen is the video recorder button. Tapping that button puts the camera into video mode, and it will begin recording right away.

To pause the recording, press the pause button. Pressing the stop button, to the right of the pause button, will stop recording video and save it. By tapping the camera icon to the left, you can return to the camera mode. If you wish to make any changes to the video settings, you must do so from the camera mode.

One of the best features of the Note 3 is the fact that it is capable of taking 4K videos for display on the new 4K televisions. These videos are very high resolution, but the Note 3 does not take them by default. To start a 4K recording, you need to open the extended camera settings and change the photo size to 3840x2160 pixels, which equates to the 4K settings.

Slow and Fast Motion

It is also possible to take slow motion and fast motion videos with the Note 3. Go into the extended settings and tap on recording mode. You can then choose fast and slow motion

45

video, as well as smooth motion. When finished with the new setting, return to the extended settings and tap on normal mode to return the recording mode to the default.

Camera Options

The camera features a variety of options, including burst shot, photo sharing, panoramic photos, and HDR.

Sharing Photos

An option called "buddy photo share" is available through the camera settings. You can enable this in the extended camera settings. Go into the first tab, the camera icon, and enable face detection. When you take a photo of a face, it will have a yellow square around it.

Tapping the square lets you choose a contact from your contact list. After that, whenever you take a photo with the Note 3, the device will attempt to recognize that contact and tag them. In the Gallery app's menu option, this will let you share photos quickly with the people tagged in them.

Location Data

The Note 3 has location tagging that can embed the GPS coordinates into the metadata when you take a photo. Go into the extended camera settings, tap the third icon on the right side, and change the location tag to on. In order to view this metadata though, you will need to have an advanced image viewer.

It is important for you to remember that tagging your photos with location data means anyone who views the photos and has the right program can obtain the GPS coordinates. For privacy and security reasons, this may or may not be ideal.

Turn the Volume Buttons into Shutter Buttons

Instead of tapping the screen to take a photo, some may want to configure your volume buttons as the shutter buttons instead. To make this change, go into the extended camera settings and click the third icon, just as when adding location data. Change volume key to camera key. It is also possible to use the keys for zoom or even to take video.

Self-Timer

The self-timer option is helpful for taking group shots. Go into the extended camera settings and tap the third tab. Change the timer to whatever duration you like, and it will take the photo automatically when the time runs out.

Mute the Shutter

It is possible to turn off the sound of the shutter easily by going into the extended menu settings, tapping on the third tab, and changing the shutter sound to off.

Using Burst Shot

The Note 3 can take a number of shots in a row, which can be helpful whenever trying to photograph scenes that have a lot of quick action. To enable the burst shot option, go into the extended camera settings in the gear icon. Change the burst shot setting to on, and then the camera will shoot in burst mode until you turn it off.

Smart Stabilization

By default, the smart stabilization mode in the Note 3 is off, but it can be very helpful when it comes to reducing motion blur. It can also help when shooting in lower light settings. Go into the extended camera settings via the gear icon and change the smart stabilization feature to on.

Taking HDR Photos

The Note 3 offers a mode that can simulate the high dynamic range and the high saturation of HDR. Tap on the mode button and then swipe to the HDR option. Tap it so that it is in the HDR mode and then take pictures as normal. Go back into the mode button to turn it off later.

Taking Panoramic Shots

To take a panoramic show, tap on the mode button and swipe to the panorama option. Tap it and then aim the Note 3 at the edge (left or right) of the panoramic scene you wish to photograph. Tap the shutter button once and slowly pan across the scene.

When you reach the end of what you want to be the panoramic shot, tap the stop button. Go back into the mode settings to turn it off.

Music

The Samsung Note 3 offers a number of different ways to play music. You could stream music through third party apps, such as iHeartRadio or Pandora, or you could buy music through the Google Play store and other online music retailers. You may also want to upload part of your MP3 collection to the Note 3 as well.

Transferring Music

To bring music from your own collection into the computer, create a folder on the Note 3 and title it "Music". The internal memory on the phone actually has a folder titled this by default, but placing it on the SD card is a better solution for those with large music collections and looking to do a bulk transfer.

Within the folder you create, you can then organize and categorize the MP3s into different folders.

After creating the folder, connect the Note 3 to the computer via a USB connection. Once the connection is established, copy your music files over to the folder on the Note 3. With many music programs, such as iTunes and Amazon's music player, it is actually possible to drag the files from their original source to the folder to copy them. This is also true of any MP3 files you have on your desktop that you want to add to the folder.

Navigating Music

At the top of the Music app are four different tabs – songs, playlists, albums, and artists. Tap one of the icons and then choose the song, album, artist or playlist that you want to hear and press play. The tabs make it easier for you to navigate through all of the music you have on your device.

Later in the chapter, we'll go over creating playlists, so you can customize what you hear.

Playing Music

After copying all of the files into the folder, tap the Music app to open it. The music is ready to play. You can listen to your music through the speakers on the phone, or you could play music through a connected Bluetooth speaker if you prefer. One of the benefits of connecting to a Bluetooth speaker is that the quality and volume of the audio is often higher.

To connect to a Bluetooth speaker, tap the menu button while in the Music app. Choose "via Bluetooth". This will allow you to configure the Bluetooth speakers to work with the Note 3. Once you configure them once, the next time you choose to play via Bluetooth, the music will start streaming through the speakers.

You do not always have to be in the Music app for the music to play. You can go into the app to start the music, and then hit the home button to go back to the home screen. The music will continue. To get out of the app and stop the music, tap the menu button and tap end.

Equalization

You can change the sound in a number of different ways, the first of which is through the equalization tool. From the Music app, tap menu, then tap "settings" and go into "SoundAlive". They have a number of different presets, as well as tools to let you tweak the sound to your liking.

The Right Sound

When playing music through the Music app, you can take advantage of the Note 3's feature to customize audio so that it sounds best to you. To customize the sound, plug in the headphones you will normally use with the device. Open the Music app, tap on the menu button, and go into "settings". Then turn on the "adapt sound" feature and tap start.

This will test your ability to hear at various frequencies, and you must follow the on screen cues to get the best results. This creates a customized setting you can choose to use for music, calls, or both.

Creating Playlists

Creating playlists is the new and faster way of making what is essentially a mix tape. To create a playlist, tap the playlists tab at the top of the screen. Then, tap the menu button, and finally tap "create playlist" from the menu.

Give the playlist a descriptive name so that you will remember what music it contains. When you are ready to add music from your collection on the phone to the playlist, tap the + sign. This will allow you to go through your music and select the songs to add. Once you've added all of the songs you want to your playlist, tap on the done button located in the upper right portion of the screen.

You can also add new songs to the playlist by tapping and holding on them. Then, select "add to playlist". You can remove songs from the playlist in a similar fashion. Tap and hold the song and then select "remove".

You can also change the order of the songs in the playlist easily. Open the playlist, tap on the menu button, and then tap on "change order." You can then rearrange the order of the songs.

Sharing Music

When using the Music app, you can also play the music you have stored on other DLNA-enabled devices that are on the same Wi-Fi network. To connect, swipe the menu bar located at the top of the screen to the right and then tap "nearby devices". Finally tap on any available devices to connect to them so you can share music to your Note 3.

Apps are certainly one of most incredible features made available to modern smartphones, tablets, and other devices. You can add new levels of functionality and fun to the device; thus, differentiating your experience from anyone else's.

Play Store

The Google Play Store is the easiest place to visit if looking for a wealth of different apps for your Note 3. There is an app shortcut in the App Drawer named Play Store. Click that app, and you can begin searching through all of the various apps available.

Browse through the selections via the on screen categories, or tap the magnifying glass in the upper right part of the screen to enter a search word or phrase to begin looking for an app.

Many apps are free, but most free apps feature advertisements within them. Some apps are available for purchase for $0.99 and up. Whenever you are considering an app, look at reviews from other users to see if there are any known issues with the app.

Staying Safe

Since the Play Store currently has well over a million different apps, it means that some of those apps may have problems, including viruses and malware. You need to make sure you are safe from these threats.

First, install apps only from trusted companies or apps discovered through trusted sources. Check the number of downloads as well. Apps with a large number of downloads and overall good reviews are likely to be safe. It is also possible to install antivirus software on the device for an added measure of safety.

App Categories

The Play Store features a wide range of different types of applications in a number of different categories. When you visit the store, whether on the Note 3 or your computer, you will see a number of different sections and tabs that help to organize and categorize the applications.

The following categories have their very own shortcut on your device as an app themselves, making it easier to access the content found in these Google Play Store categories.

Play Music

The Music tab lets you browse for songs, artists, and albums that appeal to you. You can also access the Google Play app that offers unlimited music in all different genres for a subscription fee that is currently $9.99 per month.

Play Movies & TV

You can catch up on television shows and watch your favorite movies when you browse the movie and television section of the Play Store. You can search by name, studio or network. You can buy movies and shows that you can download to your phone and other devices, or you can rent them instead.

Play Games

Mobile gaming is very popular, and you will never have a shortage of fun and interesting games to play on your Note 3. The Play Store offers games such as Angry Birds, Candy Crush Saga, and countless other options.

Play Books

Thanks to the high quality of the screen, and the size of the screen, reading on the Note 3 is actually quite easy and comfortable. The store offers new and old books in an easy to read electronic format. You can take your favorite authors with you on the go without needing to have a physical copy of the book.

To make reading even better on the Note 3, you can enable reading mode. It increases the sharpness of the text and slightly changes the color of the screen to make reading easier on the eyes. Go into device settings, device, and then display to turn it on. When you turn on reading mode, you need to specify which apps will use it.

Downloading an App

Downloading an App from the Google Play Store is very simple. Search for the app that appeals to you, tap on it and download. They will install to your device without any issue and with just a single tap since they are from the official store.

However, the Play Store is not the only place to download apps for Android devices. Other sites, including Amazon, have their own stores, and it may take a little more effort to get the apps to download and install.

Installing an App

After downloading an app from outside of the Play Store, the Note 3 may give you a notification that the install is blocked. This message will give you a tab for "settings". Tap on the tab and then tap on the box for "unknown sources". Checking this box will let the Note 3 install apps from outside of the Play Store.

You can give one-time permission to install one of these apps, or you can give permission to install apps from outside permanently. Make your decision and then tap on "next" on the following screen. The prompts that follow will then let you install the app.

Removing an App

Removing an application from the Note 3 is easy, and there are two different methods.

The simplest that will work for apps from the Play Store is to go into the store and search for the app. Select "uninstall", and it will remove the application.

The second method, which will work with all apps, is to go into settings, then tap general, and then application manager. Look for the app that you want to remove and tap "uninstall".

Chapter 9: Included Apps

While you can certainly find and download a number of apps from outside sources, the Note 3 actually comes with a robust sampling of applications already preinstalled on the phone. In this chapter, we will cover these apps and give you an idea of what they do and how to use them.

Downloads

The Downloads app is a download file manager, and the sole purpose of the app is to track the files you download from your browsers. You can sort files by date or by size, whichever you prefer. Most people will not use the Download app very often, as they receive a notification whenever they download an app. You can open the notification panel and tap on the app to open it.

However, it is possible to do the same thing through the Download app. It can also be helpful for those that want to look at the download history. It is important for you to note that the app does not move or copy any downloaded files.

Dropbox

The Dropbox app has the potential to be a very useful tool for many. Dropbox is a service that offers cloud storage, and it is compatible with many different devices and platforms, including Mac OS and Windows. You have the ability to upload and download files to and from a virtual hard disk in the cloud.

Whenever you make changes to the file, it synchronizes with all of the different devices using Dropbox, which is very helpful to ensure that all files are accurate and up to date. The app can also save older instances of the file if needed. Many will find this very helpful for keeping personal and work files safe.

S Voice

The S Voice app is the voice system for Samsung, and it actually offers some of the same types of commands and features of Google Now, which we will discuss later in the chapter. It can act as a virtual assistant, again, similar to Google Now.

Turning it on is simple. Double tap the home key and then begin speaking. After you give your first command, you can give another command by tapping the on screen microphone, or you can simply say "Hi, Galaxy". The voice can speak messages to you, read information from the screen, and more. New users can tap the question mark in the right corner of the screen to get a list of different commands that will work with S Voice.

The voice recognition application works better than it has in previous incarnations of voice recognition on smartphones.

S Health

Those serious about health and fitness should get quite a bit use out of the S Health app. Within this application you will find a GPS tracker that can be helpful while running, a pedometer, a weight diary, and a food tracker.

While the features might not be as robust as those found in other health and fitness apps, this one is free and is installed on your phone by default.

S Note

Designed to work with the S Pen, this is a powerful and useful note-taking app. It offers options for graphs and charts as well as simple notes. Upon opening S Note for the first time, you will choose a template and cover style for the note pad. The options you choose at the outset do not really matter because changing the style and settings later is very simple.

You will then need to determine whether you want to back up notes using a Samsung Account or an Evernote Account. Either of these is acceptable. Ff you never use the Evernote app on the Note 3 or on the computer, It makes more sense to choose to back up the notes with your Samsung Account.

During the first setup, you need to choose what type of input you want to be able to use with S Note. The options are S Pen only or S Pen and finger mode. This is also easy to change later, and you may want to experiment with both options to see which one works the best for you.

Once in the application, you will see a number of tools located in the upper left portion of the screen. These tools include:

Handwriting Mode – Tapping handwriting once will let you go into handwriting mode, where you can draw and write freely. By tapping again, you can change the type of pen you are using to pencils, brushes, and more.

Text Mode – Tapping this option will let you enter traditional text mode, where you type characters using the keyboard. You can change the font size, style, and color by tapping the button a second time.

Eraser Mode – When you tap this mode, two options appear. You can choose to erase by thickness or erase by stroke. The option to clear all will remove everything from the page.

Selection Mode – Tapping this mode lets you select certain parts of the sketch to change or alter. A second tap lets you make a selection with a rectangle tool or lasso tool. After making the selection, several more options will appear:
Properties – You can change a number of options here. You can resize the selection, change the colors of the lines, and change the thickness of the lines.

Transform Into – This changes the selected area into one of the following.

Shape – Choosing shape will turn the selection into the shape that it looks the most like.

Formula – This will turn the selected area into a mathematical formula. Of course, this only works if the user handwrote an actual formula on the page.

Text – The Note 3 has handwriting recognition, and that is what comes into play here. The handwritten selected text will transform into typed text.

Shape and Text – This option is available for those notes that may contain both text and some sketching.

Cut – This option will move the selected area to the clipboard. To paste the cut out area, tap and hold the S Pen in the place where you want to paste and then tap paste.

Copy – This will copy the area to the clipboard. Unlike the cut option, this does not actually remove the selection. Paste using the same technique mentioned above.

Delete – Deleting will delete the selected area entirely.

Undo – This feature will remove the last stroke or line.

Redo – This feature replaces the last stroke or line if you have removed it by mistake.

Located in the upper right part of the screen is a checkmark. This will save the note and switch over to a mode that is view only. You can go back into the editing mode by tapping the screen. This will show a pencil icon in the upper right part of the screen. Tap on that pencil icon to go back into editing mode.

You will see an insert option in the bottom left part of the screen. Tapping this allows you to add various types of content to the note. You can add the following:

Voice Memos – You can import a voice recording to the note, or you can record something new.

Images – Add an image from the Gallery, add one into a photo frame that you draw, or take a new picture with the camera.

Video – You can insert video from the Video app, record a new video, or add one from YouTube.

Easy Chart – This lets you create a table, and a variety of different types of charts, including pie charts, line charts, and bar charts.

Illustration – From the S Note's internal library, you are able to add shapes and clip art into the note.

Clipboard – Tapping this option will let you add an item that was recently on the Note 3's clipboard.

Scrapbook – You can insert items from the Scrapbook app.

Maps – You can capture and add selections from the Maps application.

Idea Sketch – You can search for sketches and add them through this screen.
Near the bottom of the screen in the center is a page selector with arrow buttons to the left and right. You can tap these buttons to turn the pages in the note. You do not have to use the arrows though, as swiping left and right will accomplish the same thing.

Tapping the center button will show thumbnails of the pages in the note. It is possible to copy pages, delete them, and re-index them from the screen by tapping on the pencil icon.

The lower right hand portion of the screen also contains buttons. The first of these buttons will toggle between S Pen mode only, and S Pen and finger mode. The second button, the gear, offers even more options, including the following.

Add Page – This option will allow you to add a page to the note. Tapping the left arrow button when on the last page of a note will accomplish the same feat.

Delete Page – Deletes the current page.

Add Tag – You can actually add keyword tags to your notes. Later, you can search through S Note using those tags to pull up specific notes quickly and easily.

Add Template – This option will let you create a new page in the note with a new template. It is not possible to change the template of a page that already exists. However, adding the template page, and then copying and pasting material to it from other pages in the note, is possible.

Edit Index – You can also add indexes to the notes, just as you would add the tags. This may be useful for longer notes.

Background – Choose a new background. You can choose a new background for the current page or for all of the pages in the note. You can use the backgrounds on the Note 3, download more from Samsung, or use your own photos.

Show Grid – Choosing this option will overlay a grid on the note, which helps with sketching. You can remove the grid through the same option once the sketch is complete.

Tapping the menu button will bring up some other options:

Share Via – Saves the note and lets you choose the pages to export in a variety of different file formats.

Edit Pages – Allows you to copy pages, delete pages, copy pages from other notes, and re-index pages.

Record Sketching – This is a fun feature that lets you record animated videos of the sketch. To start recording, tap the red circle. Tap it again to stop recording.

Unfortunately, there is no way to export these recordings, and they are only viewable through S Note.

Add Shortcut – You can add a shortcut on your home screen that takes them to your note.

Show/Hide Tools – Show all of the tools and controls on the screen, or hide them for less clutter with this option.

Save – Saves the current note.

Save As – Choose what type of file format you want to use when saving the note.

S Translator

S Translator is a translator application with the capability of translating both voice input and text input to another language. You could write something in English and then have the translator repeat the phrase in another language, for example. You could also speak into the translator and the phone will speak the translation back to you.

The translator could be a very good option to use while traveling. It features a library of 3,000 phrases as well, and many of these could be quite useful to travelers. The S translator does require a connection to the Internet to use though.

The S Translator currently features nine different languages: English, Chinese, French, German, Italian, Japanese, Korean, Spanish, Brazilian-Portuguese.

Flipboard

This application acts as a content aggregator. It combines news as well as social media and combines them into a magazine specialized to each user. Those who do not use social media as much may not get as much use out of the app as others who are on social media often.

Using Google +

Google+ is Google's social network platform, and this app lets you connect with friends, family, coworkers, and other contacts that use the network. This is just one of the many different social networking sites available, and it might only appeal to you if you know others who use the network.

However, you do not have to connect only with people you know. You can also look for communities and find others who have similar interests to theirs. It is possible to back up photos and videos at full resolution as well.

Hangouts

The chat platform for Google is Hangouts and it is a replacement for Google Talk. You can access the app and choose to text chat or video chat with contacts. Those who use Gmail will find the option to "hangout" available when logged into Gmail as well.

One-on-one conversations, as well as group conversations, are possible with Hangouts, and it offers the capability to add emojicons, GIFs, photos, and more to the conversations. It is possible to turn conversations that start as SMS messaging into video calls with up to ten other people. Even if friends aren't currently connected to a hangout, you can still message them. Hangouts are not merely available on the Note 3 and Android devices though. You can access them through computers and even Apple products.

Bloomberg+

This app offers news, stock information, and more. It even streams Bloomberg TV, and is one of the most popular applications that offer finance related news and features in the Play Store. It also comes preinstalled on the phone, so you will have access to it as soon as you set up the Note 3. Those who have stocks and need to have marketing data will get great utility out of this app, such as the ability to monitor of investments.

ChatON

This is Samsung's official messaging app, and it makes it easy to connect with friends through the free text, voice, and video messaging. You can send handwritten notes. The app even includes an in-app text translator. This lets you chat with friends who might not speak the same language.

Currently, the application is able to translate *to and from* these languages.

- English
- Chinese
- Japanese
- Korean

It can translate *from* the following languages to English.

- French
- German
- Italian
- Portuguese
- Russian
- Spanish

The application also features some fun animated stickers that are a step up from mere emoticons, and you can send videos, pictures, locations, voice memos, documents, calendars, and contact information.

The broadcast feature allows you to announce events to all of the ChatON contacts at once too.

KNOX

Knox is a security platform for the Note 3 that lets you run an encrypted version of your operating system separately from the other elements on the phone. The main purpose for this, according to Samsung, is so that a single device could act as a work device and a personal device.

When using KNOX, you will only be able to download apps from the KNOX Store. Your other personal settings, while not using KNOX, will work normally though.

The vast majority of people will have no need for enlisting KNOX. However, some who own businesses might want to try it, as it does have the ability to keep data and information secure, and it prevents commingling with personal data.

Sketchbook

While you can sketch and draw in S Note, the Sketchbook App takes things a few steps further by offering a robust set of tools. The app offers dedicated tools for sketching that can make it easy for artistic types to create stunning works of art.

The app has a flood fill tool, brush presets, smooth brush stroking, and synthetic pressure sensitivity. You can have several layers to work with for a single sketch. It is possible to import a layer from the Gallery or from the camera. You can add text, choose from a full range of colors, and save right to the Gallery very easily.

The multi-touch zoom feature is a great tool as well. You can navigate around the picture and then zoom in up to 2500% to add high levels of detail to the artwork. Naturally, Sketchbook will work with the S Pen, making it very easy to create high quality pieces of artwork on the go.

Trip Advisor

Trip Advisor is an app that can be quite handy for travelers. While it is certainly not the only app of its kind, it does come with the Note 3, and you will want to check out the options and features it has before you choose to download another app.

The app lets you do quite a few things, including finding local attractions. You can also find and book hotels, as well as flights. The app is simple to use and understand, and it has all of the features that most travelers would want.

Still, it is not the only app of its type out there. Some of the other apps that you may want to consider for travel include Priceline and Expedia. Most of these sorts of travel apps are free to download, so it makes sense to download and try several of the apps to see which ones give you the information you really need. Apps like Yelp and Urban Daddy offer more granular about local places such as restaurants, bars, and local favorites.

WatchON

The Note 3 features an IR blaster, and WatchON is an app that acts as a universal remote control. Instead of searching for and fumbling for the remote, the phone can act as your remote. The application works remarkably well with most types of televisions, including those other than Samsung. WatchON works with cable and satellite boxes as well.

Once you configure the app to your specific setup, you will see the TV guide on the phone. It can also offer recommendations based on the things that interest you. Tapping a show will give you more information about the show, and tapping again will change the channel so you can watch it.

Even though other IR remote apps are available for the Note 3, WatchON is of very high quality and, once configured, is a great solution for avid television watchers.

YouTube

Note 3 users have easy access to YouTube. You can tap on the YouTube app and log into your account, or you can start up a new account. Those who already have an account will find that your subscriptions, favorites, and more are tied to that account, so you will have access to them through the Note 3.

Some of the app's features include the "what to watch" recommendations, and adding videos to playlists and to watch later lists. You can subscribe to channels just as you would through a computer. You may also search through normal keyboard input, or with your voice. You can also share videos that you enjoy through Facebook, Twitter, email, and Google+.

Maps

Maps for the Note 3 helps to make getting from Point A to Point B quite a bit easier and quicker. The app features accurate maps for more than 200 countries, and one of the best features is the voice guided GPS navigation available right through the App. It is a nice option for walking and biking as well as driving. The app features transit directions and detailed maps for more than 800 cities, and you can access information on more than 100 million different places. The application even has street view and some indoor imagery for some buildings.

The live traffic reports and incident reports, as well as the rerouting feature help to round out the app and make Maps a standout application on the Note 3. Anyone who travels, even within his or her own city or nearby surroundings, should find this app to be immensely useful.

GPS

As mentioned, GPS is an important part of the Maps application. This is how it all works.
Tap on Maps to open the application. You can then tap the search bar at the top of the app and enter your destination. When you type in the search box, a dropdown box will appear with a list of suggestions. Choose the right destination.

In the lower right corner of the screen is a button for the route. Tap the button. At that point, the Note 3 will ask how you plan to travel to the destination. There are options in the toolbar at the top of the screen, and you can choose by car, public transportation, bicycle, or walking.

Once you choose your mode of travel, you will then see a list of suggested routes you can use. Tap on the route you prefer.

Navigating to a Destination

On the next screen, you can drag up the bottom bar to see the step-by-step directions for navigating to your destination. If you do not plan to use the text directions, you can tap the start button at the lower right portion of the screen. This will start the voice and map navigation. Then, follow the directions to reach your location of choice.

More Tips for Maps and GPS

When you are entering text into the search box, you do not always have to enter the name of a street or city. Instead, you can enter the keywords, such as hotels for example. This will show the hotels in the area.

On the home screen of the Maps app, you can pinch to zoom on the map. You can navigate to different areas of the map using one finger and moving the map around. Tapping the icon of the person to the right of the search box will open up information for you. This includes recent destinations and places you've saved, which can make navigating to those places again faster.

Swiping from the left edge of the menu will open up the menu. At the top of the menu is a button for traffic. Google collects traffic data and updates it in real time. Check the traffic by tapping on the button. Green is clear, yellow means there is some traffic, and red means there is a lot of traffic.

Google Now

Apple has Siri, and Google has Google Now, which works in a very similar fashion. Google Now is a personal assistant that comes with the Note 3 that has the ability to understand a variety of voice commands. Google Now can go a step further than what Siri is able to do, thanks to something called the card system.

Google Now will deliver information that it deems important to you throughout the day. Some of these things could include information about certain events, or even the traffic conditions. It also has the capacity to learn, so the more you actually make use of Google Now the better and more accurate it becomes at predicting what you need. You can ask and make requests of the system as well, just as users of Siri can do.

Setting up Google Now

To set up Google Now on your Note 3, tap and hold the home button. This will bring up a number of options and settings. At the bottom of the screen should be the option for setting up Google Now. If it is the first time that you are using Google Now, you will have to affirm that you want to enable it, and at that point, you will be redirected to the Google Now home page.

Be sure to have your web history turned on as well. Google Now learns about your likes and interests through your history, and it can then provide you with better and more accurate information. To turn on web history, tap the menu button and head to settings, then accounts & privacy. Make sure the web history slider is on.

Also, make sure that location reporting is on. Make sure you've also set your home and work address in Maps. This gives Google Now the information it needs to provide you with traffic data.

Using Google Now

The more you use Google Now, the more accurate and helpful it will be. You can also customize the home screen for Google Now by tapping the magic wand icon in the lower right hand portion of the screen. This will take you to a page that has the cards that Google Now uses to learn more about you and to pass along information.

By default, they have only a few cards set up, including traffic and weather. Google Now, as it learns more, will bring more of these cards into play though. In total, it has 39 different cards.

1. Active Summary
2. Boarding Pass
3. Next Appointment
4. Traffic & Transit
5. Flights
6. Weather
7. Restaurant Reservations
8. Events
9. Friends' Birthdays
10. Your birthday
11. Hotels
12. Packages
13. Location Reminders

14. Sports
15. Event Reminders
16. Movies
17. Time Reminders
18. Concerts
19. Stocks
20. Zillow
21. News
22. Research Topics
23. Fandango
24. New Books
25. New Video Games
26. Public Alerts
27. Nearby Events
28. New Albums
29. Places
30. Translation
31. Public Transit
32. Nearby Photo Spots
33. Nearby Attractions
34. News Topic
35. Currency
36. Time at Home
37. New Television Episodes
38. Website Update
39. What to Watch

If you ever want to remove an existing card, you can swipe it away. You can also tap the three dots on the right corner of the card and tell Google that you no longer want to know about such events.

Speech Recognition

Google Now also has speech recognition capabilities, which is what lets you talk to the program, as iPhone users can to Siri. To get Google Now ready to accept a voice command, you need to speak the works "OK, Google". A microphone will appear, and that means you can continue with what you want to ask or request.

Google Now is also a personal assistant, and it can do a number of helpful things for you. With voice commands, you can tell the app to set an alarm at a certain time, to schedule a meeting, to set a reminder, send a text message, navigate, and so much more. You can ask a variety of different questions, and the best way to test the limits of Google Now is to experiment.

One of the interesting features of Google Now is that it can learn your specific voice, which helps it to improve its speech recognition capabilities. You can turn on the feature by going into the voice menu and enabling personalized recognition.

Disabling Google Now

You might find that you do not use Google Now very often, or that you simply do not like it. To turn it off, tap the menu button and go into settings. Turn off the Google Now slider. **Do *not* do this unless you are sure you no longer want to use it though**. When you turn it off, it resets the features and the cards. If you turn it on again, Google Now will have to learn about you all over again.

Consider Third Party Apps Too

The apps that come with the Note 3 are very good for the most part, and they cover a variety of different functions that should suit most. However, you will also want to look at some of the third party apps that are out there. Some of the apps you might want to consider exploring and learning more about include the following: Amazon, eBay, Hulu, Netflix, Shazam, Linkedin, Facebook, Instagram, etc.

Chapter 10: Advanced Features

Thus far, we've covered the basic features that most will want from their Galaxy Note 3. In this chapter, we'll cover the more advanced options and features available for the device, which can add whole new levels of functionality to it.

Setting up a Wi-Fi Hotspot and Tethering to Your Computer

You can share the Internet connection you have on your Note 3 with another device, which can be extremely useful. Using the tethering and hot spot feature lets you use one connection to the web, through your phone, to give access to your laptop or other wireless enabled device.

When you set up one of these spots, your Note 3 becomes the router. However, you should note that when turning your phone into a Wi-Fi hotspot, you likely would have to pay for it. Most of the carriers around the country will add a charge to the monthly bill.

To set up the hotspot, you need to go to device settings, then connections, and then to tethering and mobile hotspot. Some carriers may offer this under a slightly different name, but it means the same thing and acts in the same manner.

When you turn on the hotspot, you will then need to enter a name for the network and select a security protocol. Choose SSID for the name and WPA2 PSK for the security protocol. Then, choose a password.

After creating your own network, you can connect to it from the other device that you want to use. Connecting to the new network is just as simple – and done the same way – as connecting to a wireless network at home.

Trouble Connecting?

In some cases, you might have trouble connecting. Reset the Note 3 as well as the device you are trying to connect and then start again. It should work without any problems.

Pairing with a Bluetooth Device

Bluetooth is commonly used to connect wirelessly to headsets, keyboards, mobile devices, and car stereos. The term for connecting these devices is pairing, and it is very simple to do.

Make sure the Bluetooth device is turned on, and go into the Note 3's notification panels and search for the Bluetooth toggle switch. Make sure this is in the on position to allow for pairing with a Bluetooth device. From there, you will go to device settings, then connections, and to Bluetooth.

The screen should have any Bluetooth capable/available devices listed. First, tap on the name of the Note 3 to make it discoverable. Then, tap on the name of the device you want to pair with your Note 3. This device, the one that you want to pair with the Note 3, needs to be discoverable as well.

Some types of devices are automatically discoverable, but you may have to consult the user guide for that particular device and follow the steps to make it discoverable. Once that device is on the screen under "available devices", tap on it and follow the prompts to pair the two.

If you want to rename the device, remove the pairing, or customize the connection, you can click on the gear icon to the right of the device.

Mirroring Your Screen on another Monitor

The Note 3 has a screen-mirroring feature that can let you share the device's screen with a Samsung television. The Note 3 can connect with the new wireless Samsung televisions easily thanks to AllShare support. This can be helpful when doing things such as showing videos or photos.

To use the feature, go into the device settings, and then connections, and finally screen mirroring. Check the slider switch located in the upper right portion of the screen to see that it is in the "on" position.

Of course, many Note 3 owners will not have one of these televisions. In that case, if you still want to mirror your device on another monitor, you can use the AllShare Cast Hub. This device is an added cost of about $100, but it is the only way to get the mirroring to work with non-Samsung televisions.

Glove Mode

In many parts of the country, the winters can be cold and bitter, and most people wear gloves. You still need to access your phone though, and the Note 3 has a solution for this. It is possible for you to increase the sensitivity of the screen so that even those who are wearing gloves will be able to use it.

To enable this mode, go to device settings, then controls. Enable "increase touch sensitivity". It is important for you to enable this mode *only* when you are using gloves and need it. You should make sure to turn it off when you do not need it, as the sensitivity will be far too high for normal use.

Samsung Kies

Samsung Kies is a synchronization tool from Samsung that helps with backing up and managing media. It is available for both Windows and Mac OS platforms. You need to go to www.samsung.com/us/kies/ to download the program. The program is simple to use and allows you to manage, backup, and restore your photos, videos, music, and other media on your phone.

You should perform regular backups of your Note 3 to Kies to make sure you have everything you need in case something happens to your phone.

Kies Air

Kies Air is an Android application that will offer media management options only. The app offers this over Wi-Fi, thus the name Air. It does not require any software to be installed on the your computer either.

You will find the app through the Play Store. After downloading and installing the application, ensure that the phone and the PC are on the same network to set up the devices. Follow the onscreen prompts, which will include entering a URL into your PC's browser and then entering a PIN for confirmation on both the phone and the computer.

When connected, you can then manage the Note 3's media files through your web browser. This does not have any restoration or backup features. It is for managing media files only. Some of the media files you can manage include music, photos, call logs, text messages, videos, files, and calendar events.

Air Button

In some areas of the phone, the pointer for the S Pen will start to pulse. This means that the Air Button is active on that screen, and that you can single click the S Pen button to bring up a list of recent items. Most of the time, this will bring up photos or a type of media that you can then attach to messages or in email.

77

This can help to make it far faster and easier to attach items to the message without having to go through multiple screens and getting into the Gallery. The Air Button shows recent images, and you can add them to the email or message by tapping them.

Air Command

The Air Command Menu is a way to access many of the most common functions of the S Pen quickly and easily. Whenever you remove the S Pen from the Note 3, the Air Command will pop up. You can also open Air Command by hovering the tip of the S Pen near the screen and then single pressing the S Pen button. The only time this does not work is when you are already in an active Air Button area as described above. The sections of Air Command include Air View, Easy Clip, Action Memo, and S Finder.

Air View

The Air View features lets you hover your S Pen, or your finger over various screen elements in order to make more information pop up on the screen. Even when the finger does not touch the screen, the Note 3 still has the capability to detect the finger.

A number of the different apps the come with the phone have options for Air View, including all of the following:

- Action Memo
- App Drawer
- Calendar
- Contacts
- Email
- Flipboard
- Gallery
- Messages

78

- Music
- S Note
- Video

Unfortunately, few third-party applications are compatible with this feature.

Easy Clip

The Easy Clip function makes it possible for you to copy and share parts of your screen by taking a selective screenshot. Instead of taking a screenshot of the entire screen, you can draw an area around the screen of what it is you want to capture.

You will hold down the S Pen button and trace the area for the screenshot. When you release the S Pen button, it cuts out the shape, and then you can choose one of the clipping icons at the top of the screen to rework the shape of the selection to make it look neater.

After cleaning up the selection with the clipping icons, you can then tap one of the app short cuts that are along the bottom of the screen. Some of the shortcuts that pop up are for messages, Scrapbook, email, and YouTube. Tap the one that you want to use and then you can add the screen capture easily.

Action Memo

This feature allows you to handwrite notes and even link them to other actions. Writing down a phone number and adding it as a contact immediately can be done. You can also search the Internet, Google Maps, and more with this function. You can change the Action Memo background color and the color of ink.

S Finder

The S Finder tool in Air Command works as a quick and easy means to search for content on the phone. You can enter a search term into S Finder, and it will scour every area and app of the phone to find that information. This is much faster than going through each of the apps individually. One of the best features of S Finder is that it also has the capability of going through handwritten notes and finding content related to your search.

You will enter the search term in the box and check the various filters it is using to search. You can add tags to make the search more specific as well. Going into the menu on the S Finder screen and tapping settings and "select search category" will let you choose which apps to search, which can actually speed up the search and remove the possibility of getting incorrect results.

One of the only real issues and gripes that some might have about S Finder is that it does not have the capability of searching through Gmail.

Taking Screenshots

You can take screenshots with the S Pens. In order to take a screenshot, you will just need to hold the tip of the pen against the screen for about a second to two seconds at most. This will take the screenshot and open up an editor so you can make changes to it. You can also save the screenshot by tapping on the checkmark seen in the upper right portion of the screen.

Accessing Settings

Being able to access the settings of the Note 3's main features and functions is important for all users, new and veteran alike. The settings for most of the applications and features are accessed in a similar manner, and we'll go over how to find them in this chapter.

Wi-Fi Settings

To get into the Wi-Fi settings, you can tap apps, then settings. In the network connections tab, look for Wi-Fi and tap it. If the Wi-Fi is off, you can tap the switch to turn it back on. The Note 3 will automatically look for networks in the area that are available. Find the network that you want and tap on it.

Enter the password, if needed, and then tap on it to connect. The Note 3 should be connected to the network at that point, and you can surf the web and use the device with no issues.

Bluetooth Settings

To find the Bluetooth settings, press apps, then settings, and then wireless and network, which should be right at the top. From there, tap Bluetooth settings to go to the next screen. If there is no checkmark in the box next to Bluetooth on the screen, the Bluetooth is not enabled. Tap the box to enable Bluetooth.

You can then choose from several options on the screen. Enter a name for the Bluetooth device by entering the name via keyboard and pressing okay. You can also turn Bluetooth visibility on and off. After two minutes, Bluetooth visibility turns off automatically.

Then, press the home key and the Bluetooth will be set to your preferences.

S Pen Settings

To configure the settings for the Note 3's S Pen, you should press the home button if you are not already on the home screen. Then tap on the menu button, go to settings, and then into controls. Tap the S Pen to get into the options and settings. The following are the settings you can turn on and off for the S Pen.

Turn Off Pen Detection – If this is enabled, the pen detection is actually turned off when the pen is inserted into the phone.

S Pen Keeper – When enabled, it will sound an alert and have a message pop up on the screen if the pen is moved away from the Note 3.

Pointer – When turned on, it displays a pointer on the screen when using the S Pen to hover over the screen.

Direct Pen Input – When enabled, the Note 3 will show the handwriting pad in the text input area as soon as it detects the pen.

Pen Detachment Options – You can choose how you want the display to appear when you detach the pen from the Note 3.

Pen Attach/Detach Sound – You can choose the sound you want to be played when the pen is attached or detached from the Note 3.

Motions and Gestures

You can control your phone with Phone Motions and Palm Gestures. The following is a list of the motions and gestures the Note 3 can perform.

Motions

To configure the settings for motions, tap home, menu, and then settings. Tap controls, and then motions. You can turn the motions feature on and off from there. The motion controls, when enabled, allow the following:

Direct Call – When enabled, the phone will initiate a call when lifting the device to the ear while viewing a contact.

Smart Alert – Lifting the phone receives notifications of missed calls and other messages and alerts.

Zoom – When on, tilting the phone will zoom the phone in and out while viewing pictures in the Gallery.

Browse Image – When enabled, moving the phone side to side will pan an image.
Mute/Pause – Turning the phone screen side down will mute called or pause playback when this is enabled.

Palm Gestures

To get into the settings for palm motion, press the home button, tap menu, and then tap settings. Tap on palm motion and turn it on or off. The following are the options for palm gesture:

Capture Screen – You can capture the current image on your screen and send it to the clipboard by swiping your hand over the top of the screen.

Mute/Pause – When enabled, you can pause playback and mute incoming calls by placing your hand over the screen.

Adding Accounts

When setting up the phone, you can add multiple email accounts, Samsung accounts, Google accounts, YouTube accounts, and more. The settings for these various apps need to be configured through both the Note 3 and their respective sites.

The process, while similar, is different for all of them. Follow the instructions from the provider of the account you want to add, as well as the on screen prompts from the Note 3.

Cloud

To access the settings for managing personal data, and setting up accounts as a means to upload to cloud servers, you may need to change the cloud settings on the Galaxy Note 3. To access the settings, press the home button if you are not on the home screen, and then tap menu, settings, and general. Tap cloud and then configure the options.

Tap on add account to sign into the Samsung account – or to create a new one if you do not yet have one. Once you sign in, you can sync contacts, memos, Internet shortcuts, calendar events, and more. You can also back up data, such as messages.
You can tap on Link Dropbox to sign into Dropbox or set up a Dropbox account to sync photos, documents, and videos.

Backup

To configure the settings for backing up and resetting the phone, press the home screen button, then menu, settings, and general. Tap backup and reset, which opens up a screen where you can configure your options.

Back up My Data – When turned on, it creates an automatic backup to a Google account for your data.

Backup Account – When enabled, it creates an automatic backup of your account to your Google account.

Automatic Restore – This setting, when turned on, will restore settings and other info from the backup whenever you reinstall an application.

Factory Data Reset – This will erase your information and data and return it to like new settings.

Battery Usage

To see the battery usage and settings, press home if you are not on the home screen, and then tap menu, settings, and general. Tap battery to view the battery usage for apps and services. You can tap an item to get more information about it and to see how much battery power it takes. You can also manage the power use from this screen.

You can also turn on an option to show the battery percentage on the status bar so you know how much battery power you have left at all times.

App Manager

To get into the app manager settings, you will go to the home screen and tap menu, settings, and general. Tap application manager. This gives you the option to tap downloaded, SD Card, Running, or All to view the status of the various services and apps on the Note 3.

Tapping an individual app will bring up options for it, such as stopping it from running or uninstalling it.

Security

From the home screen, once again, tap the menu, then settings and general. Then, tap security to open up the options for all of the security settings.

From this screen, it is possible to alter settings for password visibility, encryption of the device, encryption of an external SD card, and credential storage.

Conclusion

The Samsung Galaxy Note 3 is a powerful and immensely useful device that is on the cutting edge of mobile technology.

However, it is important that you learn how to use that technology to get the most from your phone. Having finished the book, you now have the knowledge needed to get the most from your new phone. While you might not need every section of this book when you first set up your phone, this book works as a great reference for recalling how to work the many features, applications, and utilities.

With this guide at your fingertips, you will always be able to get the most out of your Note 3 (just don't lose this book!).

www.ingramcontent.com/pod-product-compliance
Lightning Source LLC
Chambersburg PA
CBHW071009050326
40689CB00014B/3552